For Robin
From her god

God thoughts

Dick Williams

THE SEABURY PRESS · NEW YORK

First *Seabury Paperback* edition 1970

673-170-C-5
Printed in the United States of America

Biblical quotations: the numerous allusions to Scripture throughout the book are not meant to refer to any particular version of the Bible

CONTENTS

Part 2

Part 3

PART 1

GETTING STARTED

I'm going to try to pray.
I've got a sneaky feeling that this may be the silliest thing I've ever done.
Because I don't know whether there's a God or not.
If there isn't I'm about to start talking to myself.

On the other hand if there is a God . . .
Well, if there is a God, it would be the silliest thing imaginable not to pray.
That's just exactly the fix I'm in.

Of course I'm not alone in making this experiment.
There are thousands, millions who *do* pray.
Some pray by instinct, some pray by habit, some pray by conviction.
I suppose there are some who pray for all these reasons.
Religious 'opinion-polls' tell us that most people believe in God — in one way or another.
I know the world's a mad place. But can it be that mad?
Can so many people be so completely wrong?

OWNING UP

I haven't really tried to pray for years and years.
Not really. Not in the way that I've tried to do other things. Not so that you could *say* I'd tried.
I haven't tried to pray in the same way that I've tried to pass exams, or please my parents, or get a date even.
I haven't tried to pray as hard as I've tried to win at games.
Let's face up to it.
I haven't really *tried* to pray for years.

And now — now that I'm making the effort, I don't even know whether there is a God or not.

I do know that there's not a Heaven made of gold and jewels somewhere just out of sight — away up there, above the bright blue sky.
I do know that God isn't an old gent with a white beard presiding over everything from a golden throne.
I do know that there aren't any angels flapping about a set of pearly gates.

But on the subject of God Himself — well, yes, I've got an open mind on God.
And I suppose I've got an open mind, too, on the subject of what all those other things, like Heaven and pearly gates, stand for and represent.

WHAT DO I MEAN BY 'GOD'?

But there's something wrong here . . .
I'm using the word 'God' as if I know what it means.
And I don't.
Even if there is a God I don't know what 'God' is.
I mean I know that God must be the creator, and almighty, but while that might well mean a lot it doesn't convey all that much to me.
But I quite see that it ought to.
So when I use the word 'God'
I think I ought to be clear about at least one thing:
if it stands for anything it stands for a Being
whose greatness I cannot predefine.
To define something is to limit it. If you don't limit it you don't define it.
I talk about God as if I know precisely what He is.
I have defined Him, in a sort of way, and therefore limited him, and I've done all this before I know what He truly is like.
If there is a God then He must be unguessably greater than anything I can guess at.
This means that
in my vocabulary
the word 'God' must
stand for
a concept
capable of unlimited expansion.

EXPERIMENT

Well I'm willing to learn, if it's possible to learn.
If there's anything to learn about, that is.
How do I set about it?
O God, please show me . . .
What have I said?
I've said 'O God please show me'!
I've started.
I've said a prayer!
I was acting as if there is a God . . .
There's a thought now! If I'm to start praying I've got to act as if there is a God. I've got to assume that He exists. I've got to suppose He's here.
I've got to act on that assumption.
That means I've got to make an experiment.
I don't see how I can get around that.

I really cannot see how I *can* pray unless I act as if He exists, and is actually listening to me.

That's the whole trouble isn't it?

I've got this far before. Wanting to pray, but not wanting to *pretend* to believe in God. Because that's not honest. And I know enough about life to know that things which are built on pretence are doomed to come crashing down, sooner or later.

Let's just try to think of God's point of view. If there is a God how would *His* mind work towards mine. So far, I've just been considering things as if it's all just a matter of my mind working towards Him. But if there is a God *His* mind will be working towards *mine*, too.

What would His angle be on the difficulty I have in trying to find Him?

JUST SUPPOSE

If there is a God then He made me.
And if He made me then He is related to me in a way that nobody else is . . .
Not even my parents who gave me life, as we say.

If He made me then He must be more intimately related to me than anybody.
He must be my closest relative!
That's straightforward enough.

Well if He made me He knows all about me.
He knows how my mind works, and how it depends in part upon the state of my body, in part upon the company I keep, in part upon what I read or watch, and in part upon the things I want for myself — *that*, perhaps, most of all.

And if He knows all about me He knows how I feel about Him now — He knows all about this puzzlement and uncertainty. He understands how I feel about praying. He must be on very familiar ground with me in this state of mind, because there are so many people I know who are in the same boat as I am.

He knows my problem.
If there is a God He knows my problem. I must remember that.

And there's another thing. He's given me the brain which is asking all the questions. In fact He designed it, and he made it.

So He's given me a brain which is capable of doubting
Him . . .
Why?

WHY THE DOUBTS?

Could it be
that God wants to see whether
I'm sufficiently bothered about Him
to make the effort to look for Him?
It certainly seems reasonable that He should!
If school taught me anything
it taught me that truth is not discovered without effort.
Well God has to be the whole truth about everything.
(He has to be that — or else there can be no God.)
And if men have to sweat to find out a little bit of truth
it stands to reason,
that to find out the whole truth — namely God —
we should have to sweat a lot.
And it's more than likely that God would want it to be this way.
At school you couldn't give up trying
— not without someone finding out, that is.
The same's true of work. You have to keep up the effort or someone is bound to notice.
But that's not true about the search for God.
If you find it tough you can just pack it in
and nobody's any the wiser.

USING DOUBTS

Well if all this is true,
if things are rigged in such a way that we have to work
in order to find the truth,
then
this must be because God *wants* it that way.
And if God wants it that way
then His reasons must be good ones:
good in themselves and
good for us.
So in what way can it be good for us to have to
search for truth?
The answer must be that God wants men to *be*
Searchers — to have the enterprise to work things out
for themselves,
and
to have faith.
Yes, perhaps He likes us this way.
Perhaps we can't become properly human
unless we are seekers — men of faith.
And doubt is the thing
which can get us started.

A NEW LOOK AT MYSELF

This is interesting.
I started off trying to get my ideas about God straightened out.
And I've ended up with changing my ideas about man!

Because as soon as I try to look at myself from God's point of view,
things seem very different.
All the things which seemed a barrier to progress in my search for the truth about God
Now seem to give me the opportunity to become an integrated man:
an explorer, a searcher, an experimenter, a man of faith — well yes,
a real man.
Yes. If there is a God then *of course* He would want us to have *faith* . . .

If there is a God, that is.

But I want to be absolutely honest with myself about this.
Maybe I'm asking all these questions only to hide from myself a deep irrational desire to believe in God.
Perhaps deep down I have decided to believe in God eventually whatever path my questions take. Perhaps I'm a religious person in the grip of psychological forces too great for me to control.

I must face myself with *this* question:
am I prepared to *accept* a world, a universe, a life in

which there is *no* God?
I'm not at all sure at present whether I'm prepared to accept a life in which there is a God. That's what my thinking has really been about so far. But am I prepared to accept a world in which there *is not* a God?

I must work this out.

THE THOUGHT OF GOD

O God, ever since I can remember there has been the thought of you in my mind.
I know that I didn't make myself.
I think that there is something (*someone* perhaps) greater and more wonderful than I am, above and beyond me — and yet interested in me.
And this single thought alters the whole way I look at the world. I couldn't look at the world, or think of life, in quite the same way as I do if this particular thought were not here inside me.

The thought of you fascinates me.
Like my body itself it connects me directly with my childhood, and those great and marvellous relationships with my parents and the rest of the family.
Now that I am not a child perhaps the thought of God must be relinquished just as the sense of dependence upon parents must be relinquished.

Let's face it — I know more now than I did then. My world has expanded beyond all recognition.

But . . .
if I relinquish belief in God, if I *choose* not to believe in you, then my whole world must change. And I can't look at the world around with me with the same eyes and in the same spirit as I do even now, in this state of half belief.
For *if* there is no God . . .
If there is no God life has no rational origin, and therefore can have no destiny.

And if it has neither origin nor destiny it can have no purpose. And if it has no purpose then it has no meaning.

MAKING UP A MEANING

Of course we human beings can manufacture a meaning and a purpose for ourselves.
But if we do we must admit that it is invented by beings who have no built-in purpose of their own and that we are meaningless beings merely *making up* a meaning for ourselves.

I find no real value in that.

But above all, and more important than anything else, if there is no God then I must give up any idea that there is a loving influence, or well-disposed power, interested in the life of men.
I have always thought that there is this power.
But if there is no God then I must abandon the idea that life itself loves me. It is a blind force.

Well . . . I am willing, I am willing to accept these consequences.
Yes, I'm willing. If it is true that there is no God, then this must be my position, and these must be my beliefs.
And I am willing to accept them as the rallying points of my regrouped mind. Though what they rally me for and to I've no idea.

I am trying now to accept these consequences, and this outlook on life, which follows inevitably upon giving up belief in God.

But here's an odd thing. As I do so I find that far from ennobling me, they make me sorry for myself, on the

one hand, and pretentiously heroic about my plight on the other. Without God I'm either snivelling or swaggering.
Without God I become more concerned about myself than about others.

Is it possible for me to love others without believing in God, I wonder?

CAN I LOVE WITHOUT HAVING FAITH?

What a desperately difficult thing to think through.
I am struggling in my mind and my heart
to find out whether it is possible to love my neighbour
without having faith in God.
For my neighbour
is 'everyman' —
people —
ordinary people,
many of them unattractive people,
people who have no claim upon me at all except
that they *are* people.
Can I love them without believing in a common
Creator
who is also our Father?
Well I can develop sensual, erotic, romantic and narcissistic passions
and these spring up in a random way
which makes them for the most part haphazard and accidental.
This makes life lively, interesting and exciting.
But none of these things are love, in the sense that I am using that word here and now.

No — it seems that without believing in God
the only love I'm capable of is
that of commiseration. The sort of love which
people might have for one another as they huddle together in an air-raid shelter
waiting
for the bomb that's on its way
just for them.

This kind of love is a genuine human emotion,
in itself loveable enough,
but surely there is a lot more to love than that.

Surely there is a love which is absolute and selfless
and therefore
creative.

I believe in that sort of love.

But I cannot believe in it without believing in God.

For I know that men are selfish — or to be more personal — I know that I am selfish. And I can't believe that unselfish love can originate in a selfish person.
An unselfish love must come from an unselfish source.
And only God could be unselfish.
Therefore to believe in real love
it is necessary for me
to believe in God.

But once I do believe in God
then it becomes possible to hope
that truly unselfish love, God's love,
can find an outlet through my own life
and I can learn to love.

CHECK UP ON CHILDHOOD

Why should I distrust my childish faith in God?
I haven't lost my childish faith in my body, because the way in which I understand and express it has changed and developed.
When I became a man I put away childish things. Of course.
But I haven't put away my body, nor my family relationships.
I understand them differently, that's all.
Should it not be the same with my faith in God?

WHAT IT TAKES TO BE AN ATHEIST

Life's full of surprises.
But I never expected to have this one.
An atheist is a man of faith!
He must be!
Because a man that doesn't believe in God
believes that God does not exist.
And that is an act of faith.
It's an act of faith just as great as that taken by the man who does believe in God.
Each act requires an equivalent amount of faith.

Now this question has got to arise . . .
Am I going to be an atheist?
It's no good just asking myself if I'm going to believe in God unless I also ask myself whether I could accept the alternative positions.
So then
shall I be an atheist?
Well what does being an atheist involve?
To believe
that
life has no rational origin
that
life is the result of some great accident
that
life therefore has no destination
and, consequently, it has no meaning, except what men invent.
Atheism is a faith. It is a negative faith.
It carries with it a collection of consequences
which I *could* accept if there were sufficient evidence in

life and creation, to support them.
But I don't see that evidence, and I don't want that faith.

WHAT IT TAKES TO BE AN AGNOSTIC

I'm glad to have got that clear.
But I still am not sure about believing in God,
I suppose I'm an agnostic, really. An unsettled one, true.
But so far all I can say is that my faith comes and goes in fits and starts, so that I can talk to God one minute and wonder if He's there the next.

Perhaps there is a God. And perhaps there isn't.
The agnostic says that in the nature of things
we cannot know.

Let's think about that:
'In the nature of things we cannot know.'

That means that if there is a God then He arranged this nature of things — this 'nature of things' in which it is impossible for us ever to know.
In that case He must be a monster — if He exists.
For if God created us with these enormous questions and longings and yet arranged things so that we should never be able to know but always be tantalized — then such a God would be a monster.

The only God of which an agnostic can possibly conceive, then, is a monster like this.
The agnostic says: 'There may be a God but if there is He is a monster who has made us for perpetual frustration.'

What else is implied by the agnostic's position?
He says 'In the nature of things we cannot know.'

So he has faith, too.
He has faith *in his conception* of the nature of things.
And upon the basis of this faith he constructs a system
in which the only possible God is a sadistic monster.

The atheist needs faith to be an atheist.
His faith is that there is no God.
The agnostic needs faith to be an agnostic.
His faith is that *his* conception of the nature of things
is so right as to be the platform on which to construct
an impossible human situation and an impossible deity.

I'm glad I've stuck to this work of thinking.
I'm not an atheist. I know that.
I don't want to be an agnostic. That's certain.
An agnostic wants to keep his cake and eat it.
I can see no excuse for his presumptions.

WHAT IT TAKES TO BELIEVE

I'm left with the only alternative I can see.
To believe in God.
'I believe in God . . .'
Do I?
My logic forces me to it. But there is no feeling of faith in me.
I'm not aware of believing . . .
I have followed my reason. And it's
a bruising, narrow, uphill path that it has led me.
And it has led me to a very clearly defined spot
which very obviously is a place of
decision.
For I must decide
which of three things I am to be.

Shall I be an atheist?
Shall I be an agnostic?
Or shall I believe in God?

These are my options. They are my only options.
And I know that I cannot be an atheist.
Nor can I be an agnostic.

So — if I am to match my logic with my life —
I must believe in God.

Belief is not a trick of temperament. It is not a mood which one falls into or out of.
It is a decision, based upon reason, in which I accept the most reasonable of the only alternatives open to me as a man.

I choose God.
I believe in God.
Here, in this moment, and as a programme for life,
I do.

AFTER BELIEF — WHAT NEXT?

Now where does my reason lead me from here?
I am a part of God's creation.
This is the thing.
He made me.
I am a part of creation—as much a part of it as a rock, a tree, a glacier, a mountain range — I am a part of creation, only . . .
I am a person.
What made everything else also made me.
And I am a person.
I have a mind, will, and emotions. And it is in the combination of these that personality consist.
Whatever made me — that is, God — can make persons . . .
can make minds, will-power and emotions — just as He can also make rocks, and rivers, stars and planets.
And a power capable of creating personality must in a sense be personal.

God is a person!
Of course it would be foolish to think of Him as a person on so small a scale as human beings. But if He creates personality — if personality is His idea, and it must be — then He must have personality Himself, personality on an immense, infinite scale — but personality.
God is a person. *The* Person . . .

THE TIME OF DISCOVERY

I know I'm on to something terrific.
I can feel it with every part of my being.
I'm so full of the sense of discovering something marvellous that I'm terribly afraid I might lose my grip on what I'm thinking, and suddenly find I've lost it.
But I'm prepared to retrace the steps of my argument time and time again . . .
to slog over this same mental countryside to the same conclusions until I know my way here as well as I know my way to the top of our street.

What am I on the brink of?

If God is personal, and if God not only made the universe but also made me, then God . . .
has an interest . . .
in me!
If God is personal and I am a person then it must be possible for God to get in touch with me.
Because between persons a language can always be created.
Is there a language, God, which you use in order to speak with men?
Is there a way in which you can speak to me?
Will you speak to me?
Will you speak now?

Everything is silent. But the air is charged with excitement and expectancy.
Perhaps that's something I'm generating by myself and for myself.

I don't want to hypnotize myself. All the same, I must be open.
Nothing. Except a strange sort of peace.
A contentment that things are moving and that I'm on the right track.
That's good enough for me. Back to the hard work of thinking . . .

WHAT MADE THAT, MADE ME

Lord, I'm a part of your creation.
What made everything else also made me.
We think of the stars and the planets as strange and mysterious things.
We think of emissions of radio waves from outer space as weird and alien.
But what made them, made me.
Francis of Assissi spent time thinking of animals as his brothers.
I need to spend some time thinking about this fact — that I share a common Father with all creation.
I stand in awe of creation.
I am staggered by the distances and dimensions which astronomers mention when they talk about space.
My mind reels and my imagination boggles at the ideas we now have of the immensity of the universe.
But I am a part of the same creation as all these things.
This thought makes me feel humble — but not insignificant.
It makes me feel very, very small — but not without dignity.
It isn't a dignity which has anything to do with my own powers.
But I feel that if I am made by the One who created this vast universe, then I can be satisfied with this thought.
I am proud of my creator, because He has created so much.
And because of that I have a sense of my own value and dignity as a human being.
Save me from being big-headed, Lord. Save me, too,

from losing this sense of my fundamental value.
Because if you made me, *I'm* valuable.
Like a little pencil sketch by an old master, nothing in comparison with his great masterpieces. But precious to the one who knows, and understands. I am just a fragment of God's creation — but valuable because of my creator.

SO THAT'S WHAT I'M WORTH

So I'm valuable.
Am I valuable to you, God?
Great artists sometimes throw their sketches away! They produce them in great quantities in order to arrive at the masterpiece.
Are we human beings expendable in your creation?
Will you screw us up into balls of pain and toss us into your studio scrap heap while you pursue your grand designs?
Or are we important to you?
Do you love us?
You have given us a capacity to love and be loved.
Reason suggests that what is in us must also be in you -
In us in tiny shreds, in you in full abundance.
Is reason right?
Is there a language, Lord, by which you can speak to us —
your Great Person to us small ones?
The Bible says that you have spoken to us in Jesus Christ.
That you spoke in different ways at different times, but eventually you spoke with full authority in and through Jesus Christ.
Can this be true?

HELP ME TO UNDERSTAND JESUS

O God, help me to understand about Jesus Christ.
I've heard about Him from as far back as I can remember.
In fact I was so small when I started to hear about him that it's terribly hard to get my ideas sorted out.
A lot of my ideas are just memories of Sunday school lessons. And with them I may just be remembering what I thought the teacher was saying — and not what was actually being said.
And there were the stories at school, and the films and radio broadcasts, and the odd book I've read too. And, of course, the paintings, and the way we talked about Him at home — very reverently; as well as the way some people use His name — as a swear word.
(How odd that people use His name in such opposite ways — some bowing their heads, others using it as an oath!)
All my thoughts and ideas about Jesus are just one glorious muddle—and because I was often embarrassed as a child by being 'made to behave' when He was talked about, I'm still apt to be embarrassed when He's talked about now, because it makes me feel like a child again, and I want to be free of all that and to be myself.

But God, help me to get a clear adult picture of Jesus.
I know that it's not a bit of use being muddled about such an important figure of history.
Let me get the facts straight. Let me get a clear picture.

The only place where I can get the neccessary information is the Bible itself.

I must go to the Gospels. I must read them.
O God I'm grateful for what others have taught me in the past, but help me now to approach the person of Jesus with new eyes.
Help me to see Him as if meeting Him for the first time.
Help me, as I read the Gospels, to see Him as the first disciples saw Him, to know Him as they did, and to come to a conclusion about Him which will satisfy my intellect and my heart.

I want to know the truth. And I want to know the truth about Jesus.

O God, open my eyes.

CAN THIS BE RIGHT?

I'm staggered by what I read in the Gospels.
Jesus makes such extreme statements about Himself, and does such amazing things.
The first thing I must determine is whether the Gospels themselves are accurate.
Was He really like this? He's not very much like the Jesus I thought I knew a bit about!
Are the Gospels to be trusted?
Of course there must be plenty of people who can tell me about this. I must ask.
But let's think about it here and now. How far can I get by thinking about it?
Well, suppose the Gospels aren't true. Suppose that Jesus didn't in fact say:
'He that hath seen me hath seen the Father', 'I and the Father are one', 'I am the way, the truth, and the life'.
Supposing that He didn't heal the sick and raise the dead.
If that were so then it must follow that the men who wrote the Gospels, and the witnesses from whom they gathered their materials, and the people who circulated them, were all untrustworthy. If the Gospels as we have them aren't true it means that there was a conspiracy to deceive. And that must mean that the disciples were either crooked, or else themselves deceived.

What do I make of that?
Well, if they were crooked, it's hard to see what they were getting out of it.
They got persecuted, and, in many cases, killed for what they said they believed. Crooks don't act this way.

And what about the good they did? They did it *because* of their beliefs.
Does this sort of goodness come out of deceit? It isn't likely.
But they *could* have been deceived, I suppose.
So what if they were? That means they were gullible.

HARD TO FOOL

But they don't seem to have been gullible about anything else, and weren't weak in the head about any other matter.
Indeed, on the contrary,
they showed every sign of mental strength.
They were good men, it seems:
they were sane men it seems.
It isn't all that likely that they were deceived.
Of course I know very well that it's perfectly possible for men to be completely taken in and absolutely deceived in matters of this kind.
But it isn't so easy to deceive men of their calibre.
These men must be placed in the category of those who would be hard to fool.
And another point occurs to me.
Not only were they good men, sane men, but
they were men of differing
temperaments,
men of varying
dispositions.
No doubt some of them were highly imaginative,
men who found it easy to believe.
But by the same token it is equally certain that others
— like 'Doubting' Thomas, for instance —
were just the opposite.
But imaginative or prosaic, suggestible or doubtful,
they all believed the same thing, and that thought
stops me in my tracks.
I have to admit that
it's remarkably difficult to see them as men who were deceived.

Could it then have been the other way round?
Were they deliberately propagating lies?
I don't think that's very likely. Of course
if they thought they were doing it in a good cause, they might possibly have done so.
But it isn't a job which seems to fit their characters.
In fact it seems flatly contradictory to their attitude to life.
Besides, it is again important to remember
that
it was something which put them in immediate danger and led to the death of most of them . . .
So what am I left with?
I must face the fact that in the disciples we have good men, sane men, each of whom could check his belief against that of another person who was temperamentally very different . . .
But who believed the same thing.
I must face the fact that whatever else we may say on the subject the disciples were at least as good and as sane as I am and probably very much more so.
And that *they* were *honestly* convinced!
It follows
that if I
had been in their shoes
I too
would have been convinced.
So what about Jesus then?
If I am to take the Gospels as seriously as the first disciples did then I must take what He said and did with equal seriousness.

DOES GOD SPEAK?

If I am to know
any other person
then that person
must reveal himself to me.

Even a psychiatrist
can't learn much about a man who
will not speak.
Therefore I don't suppose that
even the most brilliant intellect
can
by its own best efforts
learn anything very much about
God.

For God is
a person.

Therefore if I am to know Him
God must speak . . .

Does He?

Quite clearly that's what the Bible claims to be all about.
It is a product of the faith that God does speak.
It claims to be the record of that speech.

I must read it.

WELL, LET'S READ THE BIBLE

Well here is my Bible, Lord —
the one I was given when I was eight years old
as a Sunday School prize, the one with
coloured pictures:
this plump, sturdy, hard-backed book.
I open it and notice again
the smallness of the print,
the double columns, the indentation which marks
the beginning of each verse, and the sprinkling
of words printed in italics . . . Here it is,
looking up at me with all its familiar strangeness.
It's all very familiar
and yet I am a stranger to it, Lord.
For it is a book I haven't read. Oh yes, a dozen or so of its thousand pages, perhaps. But only enough to have got it fixed into my head that this is not for reading.
And so I have to look at the table of contents to find out which book is where.
And how confusing it is as I try to work through it. It's as hard to get through as an Amazonian jungle. And the beautiful old English is not compulsive reading. Particularly in this small type and funny lay-out.
And every time the words begin to crawl across my mind I can hear the echo of the Vicar's voice, and see the choirboys giggling in their robes,
and smell the straw in the kneelers at church, and feel the clammy cheeks of an old hymn book — the sort that's stuck together with elastoplast.
And I find that all these things are filling my mind, and not what the passage is actually saying.
Lord, help me to read the Bible.

Help me to grasp the pattern of its composition, and see what its different parts are,
and understand it fully, so that it becomes
mine.

And, Lord, here too is this new translation of the Bible, looking like a detective novel, all glossy, bright and with-it.
I bought it at the Railway Station this afternoon.
And as I look at it, it reminds me only of the past few hours,
And the other paper-backs
about sex and crime
from which I took it, while people jostled past me
for the train.

How different they look, these two books —
but yet they are the same.

O Lord I thank you for them both. Because I thank you for *it* . . .
the Bible.
This is the book which tells us of Jesus and I
want to know all I can
about Him.

SO THIS IS THE CHRIST

As I've been reading and thinking
about Jesus I can't help boggling over what He obviously thought of Himself . . . what He considered Himself to be.
Obviously,
and beyond all doubt,
Jesus Christ considered Himself to be the Son of God in some way that other men are not.
He certainly claims to be unique.
He even seemed to think that He existed before all creation — that He was around before the first star pricked the darkness of space.
He believed that He was the only way to God.
He said that we have to eat His flesh and drink His blood in order to come alive properly.
He said that He could forgive sins and make eternal life available to human beings here and now.
I am amazed and staggered by what Jesus said about Himself.
It shatters my childhood conception of Him, just as new wine is supposed to burst old bottles.
He is so much bigger, greater, immensely more powerful and dynamic.
Disturbingly so in fact.

What on earth am I to make of Him?
How am I to think of Him?

If anybody walking the earth today said things like that about Himself in my hearing
I'd almost certainly think him to be insane.

So I can understand the point of view of those who totally opposed Him when He was on earth.
Of course, I might not have done so if I could have seen and heard Him as He actually was.
But still, I can understand them in theory.

I never could before.

WAS HE CRACKED, CROOKED, OR CORRECT?

Was Jesus mad?
That is the sanest question I can ask at the moment.
How far can commonsense get me with this question here and now?

I shall need to talk this over with someone. Perhaps I shall need to read books.
But I must think about it for myself. And think about it now.

Well it would be common sense to say that anyone who *is* off his rocker isn't going to be a lasting force in the world. None of the world's crackpots, so far as I know, have had a lasting effect.
Certainly not a lasting effect for good.

Nobody finds a continuing source of help and guidance from what maniacs have done and said. Religious maniacs don't do much good,
from what I hear.
Jesus, however, seemed to do a lot of good.
And although the church has made its mistakes
this seems to be due to the failure of Christians to follow Christ.
Indeed His teaching has been consulted by enormous numbers of people for two thousand years.
And millions study His words today.
So on that count He doesn't appear to have been insane.

In addition to that, the crackpots don't seem able to

cope with the real problems and difficulties of life. They live in a dream-world — presumably because they can't cope.

But Jesus coped all right.
He appears to have coped as no man did before, and as no man has done since!
Jesus was very much concerned to live in the real world, very much concerned to dodge illusions, too.
That is certainly reasonable evidence — it is in fact almost proof — that Jesus was quite sane.

But if He wasn't insane, perhaps He was a deceiver, making a living out of a credulous bunch of people, or trading on their desires only in order to inflate His own ego.

If this were so it's hard to see why He should have gone so willingly to the cross. It's pretty obvious that He could have avoided arrest if He'd wanted to. He could have arrived at some sort of compromise with the Jewish and Roman powers and still have been a sought-after personality.

But there it is. The cross.
A crook wouldn't willingly die such a death, nor would he die it in the way Jesus did: 'Father forgive them . . .'
Fancy being able to say that!
Besides, the things He did, the laying down of His life day by day in the service of others, all this isn't the work of a bad man.

I can't honestly think that He was either mad or bad.

And if He was neither of those two things then . . .
He must be what He said He was.

God. God the Son.

HE MUST BE RIGHT

This is fantastic.
I don't know how or where to begin even to consider this thought.
Jesus is God.
Jesus — a man . . . God: the creator of this fantastic universe, and of all life.
Jesus is God!

So far as Jesus is concerned it's a matter of believing that, or else of having done with the thought of Him for good.
It'd be a question of believing that or having done with Christianity once and for all . . .

This is it.
This is the crunch.
All my thinking has been along a collision course with this man Jesus.
This is the collision . . .

I'm drawing back from my experiment in prayer now.
I must take stock — look around, get my breath back.

The first thing that springs to mind is that I've got a terrific excuse for packing the whole thing in.
It's so easy to say that it's impossible for Jesus to be God.
Therefore it's perfectly easy to have the most respectable reason for packing in Christianity.

IS IT REASONABLE?

The only thing which weighs with me is this:
I have got to this fantastic position by being reasonable.
If I say 'It is impossible for Jesus to be God', is that a statement of reason?
No. If God is almighty — that is, if God is God — then it would be *un*reasonable to say that He could *not* enter into His creation as a man.
It *is* unreasonable to think that a man can become God — because man is so much less and other than God.
But it is highly reasonable to suppose that God can become man, because God created man, and can do whatever fits in with His own will and character.

If God should choose to become a man then reason as such can find nothing to say against it.

To say it's unreasonable is to prejudge the matter.
It is to be like the old country bumpkin who heard travellers' tales of giraffes and said 'It's impossible — such an animal could not be!'

It was ignorance, and the instinct based upon it, which made the bumpkin say that it was impossible.
And the conservative instinct which springs from ignorance always has a great show of reasonableness to our mind. I know that.

Reason can never oppose the idea that God became man.
So
did He?

Is Jesus God?
If He is then, as I pray to God, I am also praying to Jesus.
Lord Jesus . . .
Didn't Paul say that on the road to Damascus?
What did he say?
'Lord . . . what wilt thou have me to do?'

I'll say the same.

LORD JESUS COME IN

Lord Jesus
I have been reading the Gospels
And re-reading them.
I see you now more clearly, more fully, and with more realism than ever before.
You are the Word of God,
God's language to men.
And more than His language—His complete statement of Himself in human terms.
In you all that God has to say about life has become flesh and blood.
In you God's whole attitude to everything has become a Man.
You are God incarnate.
You are all I need to know about God.
You are the Word of God, and I read that Word by looking at you.

'Behold I stand at the door and knock . . .'

O Lord I'm empty,
But I know that life is designed for greater things than the mind alone can grasp.
For it is made by you and it is made for you.

'Behold I stand at the door and knock. If any man hear my voice and open the door . . .'

O Lord the door of my heart is open to you.
The building of my life is open to its architect, designer, engineer, builder . . .

Be more even than these, Lord; be
its owner.
My heart is open to you.
Come in!

'Behold, I stand at the door and knock. If many man hear my voice and open the door, I will come in.'

Thank you, Lord.

Thank you for entering my life, and thank you for the spirit of glad consent which you have given me.

You have come to me many times before, from childhood until now.
But you have come uninvited by me. You have come from Fatherly goodness.
Thank you now for having made me willing to invite your coming.

You have waited for this moment. I think that I have waited for it too, without always knowing what I waited for.

Thank you for entering my heart.

Make it your own.
My heart is now the colony of your spirit.
Live within me. Grow within me.
And change the customs of your colony
to suit yourself.

PART 2

'GOD IS LOVE'

Thank you God for loving all creation equally,
and for loving me as a part of it.
I thank you particularly for putting beyond all question the fact that it is your nature, character and disposition to love.
Thank you, therefore, that your love for me does not depend upon my deserving or my worthiness.
It is such a relief to know that you love me,
not because *I* am loveable, but because *you* are love.
I thank you for helping me to see
that my value consists in these two facts:
that you made me, that you love me.
I know now that just as I did not have to do anything in order to be created
Neither must I do anything in order to be loved.
I accept completely the fact that you love me unchangeably and forever:
I accept this as one of the given, unalterable things of life like the sun which shines whether we deserve it or not.
'God is love.'

GOD IS TRUTH

'The righteous Lord loveth righteousness.'
Jesus said, 'I am the truth.'
'God is judge.'

Teach me Lord to rejoice in your righteousness.
For I am glad that you are the truth.
Truth is the spring-board
of creation —
the launching pad of all that is.
And you, O God, are truth.
And righteousness is truth in action.
O God teach me to rejoice in your righteousness.

Thank you for being hostile to everything evil in the world and thank you for being hostile to the sin which is in me.
But thank you above all for loving me while hating my sin; for being able to save me, and still be true to yourself.

Thank you for being the God of truth.
Thank you for being the God of love.
Thank you for being both in one
and for showing how love and truth
belong to one another, and
are united in the nature of God,
jointly revealing something
of what you are.

GOD IS LIGHT

Something inside us
seeks the light like
flowers thrusting towards the sun.
Light is the dimension into which
all that we are potentially
can expand
to perfection.

We thank you Lord, that you are light —
drawing out our hearts and minds and wills towards yourself.

This growth towards the light is not always easy because it is the nature of light to reveal all things
and make them clear and plain.
And we who are called to live in the light are called to live in an awareness of ourselves in which
there is no self deception.
We are called to live a life in which there are no secrets between ourselves and you,
a life in which we are transparent, and open, and entirely without pretence in our relationships with each other.

O God, you are light.
We thank you for the light, and for the great relief and liberation which comes to us as we live in the light.
But because of our sins we are also glad
that you who are light, are also — in entire completeness — love.

GOD IS SPIRIT

When we talk about 'Spirit'
We either think about 'Ghosts' or else
nothing.
Nowadays we have more less debunked ghosts. So
All that is suggested by the word
'Spirit'
is
nothing.
So when we hear about the Holy Spirit
we are apt to think of a sort of
Holy Nothingness . . .
A thought which is either baffling or else
just plain ridiculous.
But it wasn't a Holy Nothingness which
filled the disciples on the Day of Pentecost.
It was a power which changed the world; a power
which continues to change it.
And when the Bible tells us that
God is Spirit
then it becomes quite clear that I have to rescue this
word 'Spirit'
from the limbo into which, in my vocabulary, it has
sunk, and start using it as a *new word.*
After all 'God' has become a new word in my language,
because
God has become something new in my experience.
And if God is Spirit, it follows
that 'Spirit' must become something new too.
And it has in fact —
without my having become fully aware of it —
already done so.

God is Spirit.
And God made all things.
This of course means that God is greater than all things
and so the Spirit
which is God
is also greater than all things.
Therefore all matter, all energy, all life, all creation
comes from that Spirit which is God.
It is that Spirit from which all things spring. It is related to creation as cause is to effect.
God is Spirit.
So, whatever is mightiest in Creation
this Spirit is mightier.
And when we talk about the 'Holy Ghost' we are talking about this.

THIS IS CHRISTIANITY

God is love,
God is truth,
God is light,
God is Spirit.
This God became a man, and dwelt among us, and we beheld His glory.
And to as many as received Him, to them gave He power to become the sons of God:
children of love,
children of truth,
children of light,
in whom His Spirit dwells.

This is Christianity.

FINDING THE FAMILY

Lord God
I have made a thrilling discovery.
I have found others who know you in the same way as I have come to know you.
I have met others in whom you live.
I have found Christians.
I have found the Church.
And I know that we *belong* to each other, because we belong to you.
We are members one of another, and together
we form the Body of Christ on earth,
to express, state, articulate, make real to others, and to the whole creation, the central truth about the whole of life — that
Jesus is Lord.
Thank you Lord for the Church — for all other Christians.
Thank you for living in our hearts and, through binding us to yourself, binding us to each other.
Lord I belong to you. Lord I belong to them.

FINDING THE FAMILY'S FAULTS

It has been a wonderful thing, Lord,
to discover your family the Church.
So wonderful in fact that it is tempting to think of it as the perfect society.
But of course that would be silly.
How could it be?
For I am a part of the Church, and I
am not perfect.
The imperfection of the church should cause me no surprise:
since I know that I can be touchy,
Why should I expect others not to be?
Since all too often I want to be the centre of attention, why shouldn't I be prepared to find the same fault in others?
Since I worry about what other Christians think about me rather than of what God thinks, or the world needs, why should I be surprised when the Church is timid and conservative?
Since I have found what delight there is in basking in the praise of others, why should I suppose that every Christian leader should be immune from the temptation to regard his position in terms of his right to privilege,
rather than his responsibility for service?
The shattering thing is
that all these are the problems of heathen men and women.
And yet we find them in the Church too. Because
we take them with us.
And yet

Christ is at work in us
teaching us to know ourselves,
making us able to accept one another as each one actually is, just as God accepts us.
For He accepts us
while we are sinners
with nothing to commend us except
our wish to be forgiven.
But that
is what makes God's family, the Church,
such a wonderful thing.
For it is made up of sinners who know themselves
to be sinners who turn to God,
and who, in that knowledge,
accept one another
in love and humility.
There is glory in this.
And since He who has begun a good work in us will finish it
we can all look forward together to the day when God will have created
the perfect society.
And that will be glory beyond imagining.
For then we shall be
changed from glory into glory.
'Finish then thy new creation!'
O God, I thank you for your Church
as it is;
as it shall be.

THE HOLY COMMUNION

Bread and wine.
Food and drink.
Jesus took these in order to express
the majesty of God's love;
the mystery of His coming;
the great assault of good upon evil; the fierce attack of evil upon good; and the victorious tragedy of His own death.

Bread and wine, food and drink — these to be
the silent preachers of salvation, and our at-onement with God.

Before I come to Communion today I think about the bread and the wine.
I know that there are some things which are beyond the power of words to express. Surely that is why
He took bread, and broke and gave it!
Words can change their meaning, and there is
the constant need for retranslation.
But with this action Christ spoke to men of every tongue and in all ages.

'God was in Christ reconciling the world to Himself.'
Now this mighty mystery is shown to us so simply as to seem an understatement.
The symbols — bread and wine; the sign — breaking and sharing, giving and receiving. This gift is
to be seen, to be accepted,
by the rebels who return.
Lord you are our life.

And your life in us must feed upon its source.
And so we come.
And as I take and eat, take and drink, the broken body, the poured out blood,
may the pride which is within me
break, bleed, die;
and I myself be buried with Christ: now and here, as I eat and drink my death.
Then having died
begin with Him the resurrection life.

O Jesus the bread and the wine remind me that you are within me.
And as surely and as simply as the bread and wine strengthen my physical life
so their meaning strengthens my response to you, and fills me with your fulness.
Today
you have touched my senses and my soul has answered.

You are in me forever,
you are in me more fully than ever,
and I am united with all your children everywhere;
we are one body, your body,
and we offer to you ourselves to be precisely that,
in thanksgiving.

SUNDAY

O God,
this is your day.
I know that all the days are yours
because Time itself is your idea, your invention, your creation.
But this day is your day in a special sense.

It stands for the seventh day of creation —
the era of peace,
that peace which flowed from your heart and flooded your new creation as you beheld it
perfect:
it stands for the moment of high delight which was yours when you saw the work of your hands and were satisfied:
it stands for the era when, after unimagineably intense involvement with your creation,
you stood back
at peace
to enjoy it
to possess it
to let your spirit flow over the whole of it
as it spread before you in all its perfection.

And so I too, on this day, your day,
with all your people everywhere, stand back —
stand back from the rush and toil of daily life —
stand back to look at you afresh
and to look at your creation
so that we may see even our own selves with new eyes
and fresh understanding as we stand back,

as we rest,
as we worship.
And this is your day, God, for another reason.
For while it reminds us of the last day of creation it also represents the day on which Jesus rose from the dead, the first day of the week, the first day of new life.
For He rose to start a new life for all who put their trust in Him.
He rose to create a new humanity.
And so this day stands for the birth of a new humanity,
the possibility of a new beginning,
the fact of the Resurrection.
And with this special day, and its special reminder, and its special truth, every week begins.
And so
each week, every week, begins in hope — with old things passed away, with all things become new,
as at the creation,
when you, God, stood back and saw all things, and beheld that they were very good.

O God, this is your day. It stands for a 'last day', and it stands for a 'first day'.
And it reminds us that when the old creation shall be no more, the last day will become the first day of the new Heaven and the new Earth.

Thank you Lord for your day. For what it means. For what it provides.

SPEAKING IN PUBLIC

Lord I have never spoken in public before
about my Christian faith.
Tonight is the night I begin.
And I begin with everything on my side except my nerves.
For the situation itself is designed to be on my side. It is artificially contrived by the Church —
a well-organized meeting by a well established
community of highly respectable people
in a building not likely to be invaded by trouble-makers.
Tonight everything is loaded in favour of what the speakers have to say.

It will not be like Peter's job on that day of Pentecost when the streets of Jerusalem were his pulpit and all the world was ranged against the murdered Christ.
But neither, for that matter, will it be totally dissimilar.
For there will be people there to listen — real people, with real lives to live — Christians who need the challenge of another life, even if only of my own poor one, and hesitating, uncommitted people — half-believers, who very well might be encouraged by my own weak example to make their act of faith —
provided that I am
honest enough to say what Jesus means to me.

Therefore, Lord, help me to be honest.
And I shall help myself to be honest too, for
I shall imagine that in the audience are all the people who know me as I am: my family, my workmates, my Christian friends.

UNDERSTANDING MY DOUBTS

Why should doubts come now of all times?
I have reasoned things out, and seen the issues clearly.
I have decided to have faith, and act in faith.
I have gladly given myself to you.

Why then these doubts?

Shouldn't they have disappeared when I made my decision?
Shouldn't that wave of great peace and joy, that sense of destiny and fulfilment which came to me then, should not these have dug the roots of doubt out of my mind for good?

Or could it be that these doubts are drawing my attention to some part of my mind where there are problems which I haven't faced and dealt with yet.
Are they like a toothache which registers at some point remote from the actual source of the trouble? — like pains in a leg which indicate an injury to the back?

If so, Lord, help me to trace the doubt to its real source.
Help me to seek out the root causes of my doubt,
and help me to do it fearlessly
in the knowledge that I can do nothing against the truth:
that what is true will remain true however radical my questioning may be.

Or are these doubts
just excuses which I provide for myself

(from the subconscious resources of hidden selfishness)
in order not to do something which I know I ought to
do but do not wish to do?

Or are these doubts reminders
sent by God Himself
who wishes His children to be men of faith:
men for whom faith is not just assent, not just an act,
but a continuing
lifelong
activity?

Thank you Lord for these doubts.
Teach me, through them, all that I need to know.
Make me, through them, all that I need to become.

JEKYLL ON SUNDAY

Lord what a difference there is
between being a Christian on Sunday, and being one on Monday.
In the warm fellowship of a church gathering I am bold, confident, and have a pretty good supply of the right things to say.
At work on Monday, amongst those who can't or won't understand, amongst those who can't or won't believe, amongst those who like to 'take the micky',
my confidence vanishes, and I become cautious and uncertain.
My timidity seems to be in an inverse ratio to my boldness of the previous day.
So I feet a bit of a fraud — a sort of religious Jekyll and Hyde:
Jekyll on Sunday and Hyde on Monday.

I don't like to be thought of as being the odd man out!
That's why I am so much to the fore among the group at church.
And it is for precisely the same reason that
I curl up inside on a Monday morning when the swearing starts, and the leg pulling begins.

Is there any way in which to be simply
myself? Myself as I want myself to be. Myself
the same in all situations and circumstances.

Lord teach me how to do it. You know how it's done, for you did it when you were on earth.

MY JOB IN LIFE

'God said unto them, "Be fruitful — have dominion." '
Jesus said: 'Follow me.'

You made my life, O God, and I have given it to you.
Show me what to do with it.
I don't want to see the whole pattern, of course. Just a bit at a time, just enough to be going on with. That will do.
But I cannot hide from myself the knowledge that some big decisions are going to have to be made along the way.

It's fairly clear to me that
the greatest act of selfishness open to me,
and the most negative and destructive decision I can make, is to keep you, God, out of my thinking about my job, and my career.

It may be that half a century or more of inventive and creative labour lies before me.
All that can be God's
and if it is God's it will be for the good of men,
and also for my own true fulfilment.
Equally, of course, it all might be devoted simply to myself, to the benefit of no-one, and to the increasing deformity of my own character. Help me in these early decisions.
For the path I take today
is bound to dictate where I shall find myself tomorrow — and a journey of a thousand miles begins with one step.

Lord, what do you want me to do?
Help me not to act emotionally.
Help me to assess my capabilities, my resources, my opportunities.
But as I try to be rational
let me not disregard my emotions, because I can learn something from them too.

But as I consider my own personal wishes and desires (for they are surely a part of the evidence I must consider)
help me not to be hasty.
Yet, also, Lord, save me from postponing decisions until I am no longer able to decide
and find that by drifting I have committed myself blindly to a course which might imprison me for life.

Help me to take advice, and give it due weight.
Help me, also, to understand myself, so that in giving due weight to the views of others, I may not give to them undue weight and so be ruled solely by another man's estimation.

When I face the possibilities before me, Lord, give me the mind of Christ.
Whatever the job may be, however ordinary, however limited, however extraordinary, however imponderable,
May I share it fully with you, and do it your way.

Lord there is something you want me to do with my life.
Help me to find what it is.
Help me to do it.

READING THE BIBLE

Lord,
Here is my Bible.
Here is this quiet room.
Here is this quiet time,
and here am I.
Open my eyes; open my mind; open my heart:
and speak.

AFTER READING A PASSAGE FROM THE BIBLE

Thank you Lord
for what you mean by this passage.
I believe I have the gist of it.

I know your truth is like a seed which will grow.
Let this kernel of meaning, this germ of truth,
which you have put into my mind
also penetrate my heart
and may it grow and expand in both,
so that, through mind and heart alike,
it may direct my will,
and shape my life.

A MORNING PRAYER

Good morning, Lord.
I must go to work, soon. I have
five minutes
before they expect me downstairs.
I should have got up earlier. Help me to have
longer tomorrow.
But now
help me to make the best use of the time I have got.
Five minutes, God.

First, I thank you for last night. For sleep.
And for security, peace and refreshment. And yes, Lord, I thank you for its comfort and warmth, too.
I'm truly grateful
for the mighty miracle which breaks life up into manageable proportions.

And I thank you for your love
eternal, unchanging — more dependable than the sun which rises to make this a new day.

And I ask you, Risen Lord,
to enter my heart and mind anew, now, fully,
expanding and enlarging my mind and heart,
preparing me for today.

And I ask you God, to look after each member of this family, and care for them as completely as I ask and trust you now to care for me.
Make me ready, God, for what the day will bring.
Save me from getting mixed up about what's right and

what's wrong. Keep me quite sure about the difference.

Help me to do your will.
And whatever happens, good or bad,
help me to take it the right way.

Help me to love you in reality and truth
and may all things serve your purposes.
For if they do I can be happy in the knowledge that,
one way or another, and in your own good time,
they will be for my own good too.

And now I'm off.

Amen.

A PRAYER LATE AT NIGHT

Don't let me fall asleep just yet, Lord,
I'm tired out,
but I want to say thank you.
I want the memory of today — with all its ups and downs —
to have time to take shape in my mind
and as it does so
to be offered now in simple gladness
to you.

And now, Lord, thank you.
Thank you for your unchanging love;
for correcting me when I've gone wrong:
and for giving me joy when I have obeyed you.
Thank you for the people I've met,
and for those I've been so fortunate as to help.
And if I have sown the seed of your word in the hearts of others, then I'm glad, and rejoice to leave it to your care.
And in your care I leave my sinful self. Lord forgive me.
And now
I commend my loved ones to you, with all my heart,
in the same act, and with the same totality,
as I also commit myself.

Amen.

AT THE START OF A DIFFICULT DAY

Life gets tedious.

Today
is far too much like
yesterday
and the day before yesterday,
and
the day before that.
I don't want to get on with the business of living
today.

I know what jobs I've got to do
and I don't want to do them.
I know what people I've got to meet
and I don't want to meet them.
I know the places I've got to go to,
and I don't want to go there.

As I look at them
the tiniest duties of the day
become enormous.
Today
I feel beaten before I start.

Did you ever feel like this,
Jesus?

That's funny!

As soon as I ask the question
something is different.

There's a shift in the perspective
of what is visible
as I look at
today.

For now I see that
today
contains Christ.
He has become a part of this terrible day.
And the day is not so terrible.
He has gone before.
Already He is present in the midst of everything
that makes it dreary —
the dreariness begins to disappear.
It's as if the sun is beginning to shine.

THE CHURCH WE GO TO

Lord, I thank you for this church
where
week by week
we worship you.
I thank you for all that has caused it to be built here:
for your love,
your Son,
your Spirit,
your people
and their ministry down the years.
For the missionaries who first preached the gospel in this land,
and in this corner of it. For
the first congregation to gather in this region
and for the eventual resolve to build this place.
I thank you for the architect who designed it,
for the artists who added to it,
for the men who constructed it,
for the people who paid for it,
and for the great company of those who,
in different generations,
have worshipped within its walls, and
for those who do so now.
I thank you for the ministers of
Word and Sacrament
who have toiled here, and for
the thousands of hours of prayer, study and thought,
which have been directed
by them
into the life blood of your family here.
I thank you for those who write and play and sing

the music,
and for all who keep the building sound, and clean,
and warm.
And, together with them, bless
all
who come here to worship
today.
May 'the glory of the Lord
fill the house of the Lord'
and may the district in which it is set, and
for which we are responsible to you,
receive,
through this place,
the Word of the Lord.

ON GOING TO A DIFFERENT CHURCH WHERE I AM NOT AT HOME

Oh dear! I didn't like the way they 'did' things
at that church.
I was so distracted by the differences between
that form of service and the one I'm used to that
I couldn't concentrate on you at all.
Instead of feeling full of praise for you
I felt full of annoyance with the church
and its ways.

Was I right to feel that way, or was I wrong?
Was that sense of aggrieved indignation a Christian feeling?

The two great commandments are: to love God above all; to love my neighbour as much as I love myself.

What do these teach me about how I felt at that service?

Was it love for God which made me feel that they were giving expression to a false interpretation of Christianity?
If a wrong understanding of God's being and His ways were being put across there then of course I was right to be disturbed.

But before I hasten to criticize I must love these neighbours as much as I love myself. I must ask myself
this question:
Do I really know what this form of service actually

means to those who are used to doing it this way?
What it meant *to me,* there and then, I believe to be wrong.
But did it mean *to them,* what it meant to me?
If I am to love them as much as I love myself
I must try to see this service from their point of view,
see it through their eyes, and put myself,
as completely as possible,
in their place.

Only when I know what it means to them can I have a real idea of whether it is true to God's being and His ways.

And of course, I freely recognize, that
if these people were to come to our church,
the very fact that I am upset by their service must mean that they would be upset by ours.

That is bound to be true. And if that were to happen I should very much wish that they would see our form of service through our eyes, and also enter into it, in the spirit in which we ourselves do.
I should want *them* to love *us,* as much as they love themselves!
So help us, Lord. Help us not to worship our own outlook but to worship you.
Help us to love you, and so to love one another.
If I can't try to see my brother's path to God I can't love him very much, and if I don't love him very much, I can't love you very much either.
And yet I want to.

AFTER ATTENDING A NEW FORM OF SERVICE

How much I enjoyed
this new form of worship,
Lord.
It shed new light on old truth.
It has debunked the cockiness
which was beginning to sit upon my self-assurance.
It has made me a learner once more, for
it made me think.
It made me feel.
It has rescued my mind from
forms of worship which have become so familiar as
almost to be deprived of meaning.
Thank you so much for the minds which have reminted
the unchanging truths of the gospel
so that to encounter them in this way
is to experience their greatness anew.
I feel renewed and liberated.
And I thank you, too,
That after experiencing this change, I am able,
strangely enough,
To see unsuspected meanings in the old form of service
which I was beginning to think that I knew all about.

PRAYER FOR A SICK FRIEND

I want to pray for . . . who is sick.
I don't want this prayer to be mere empty words.
I want it to be a real prayer.
I want it to make a difference to him.

And so I think of my friend now,
and thank you for him.
As I do so I notice the difference which illness has made to him. It has taken away all casual surface reactions to people and things. And therefore
it has revealed what remains.
Now I can see how his attitude to life stands fast and improves while his body is weak,
and because of these things I find that I know him better than before. I thank you Lord, for the help which you are giving him in his illness. I thank you for helping him to cope with it — I thank you that he accepts it and also rises to meet its challenge and attack.
I want to be alongside him in my prayers.
May he be aware that we are for him, and with him.
And whatever his deepest needs are today, I ask you to meet them.
Lord you made him.
Therefore you have the power to heal him.
I ask you to do so, through Jesus Christ our Lord.

FOR THE CONVERSION OF A FRIEND

I thank you Lord for my friend: For the years in which
we have enjoyed each other's company —
the way we spark each other off in
conversation and recreation —
for all the attitudes and out-looks we have in common,
and for all that I have received and learned from him.

I pray that we may also have in common
the greatest thing of all:

I pray that he may come to know you
through Jesus Christ our Lord.

But I recollect
that I was brought to know you willingly,
with nobody bringing pressure to bear.
And I realize his need to find you in the same way.

I recollect also the people who spoke the right words
to me at the right time.

And bearing both these things in mind
I pray that in my friendship with him
I may be your servant.
Show me when to speak and how to speak.
And show me also when to be silent.
And I pray that the Holy Spirit,
who found a way to turn me round and
find life,
may also work the same great work
in him.

A PRAYER ABOUT FALLING IN LOVE

Dear God,
I know that love is not a rational thing.
It does things to us which
upset the calculations and arrangements
of everyday life.
Our reactions to everything, good or bad, are
exaggerated in the extreme, so that
we are either on the crest of a wave, or
in the valley of despair. But the happiness of it
is so utterly delightful
that it must come
from you.

I wouldn't have it otherwise, Lord.
But I know that there are dangers here which are
unguessable, and enormous. For all around us
there is evidence
that falling in love is no guarantee of happiness,
and can end in the wreckage of life.

And yet it is a part of the life of everybody, a part
of life as you designed it, God.
Therefore
while we are awake to its dangers we do not want to be
afraid of it, either.

Help us then, O Lord, in this relationship.

May we not be ruled by our feelings,
whether they be feelings of delight or of despair.
Help us instead to serve you and set you to be our ruler.

Help us to abide by the simple laws which you have
given us for our guidance, from your love.
And if marriage should clearly emerge in our lives
to be your will for us
then let the great powers and delights of our love
strengthen still further our desire to be your servants.

WHEN FRIENDSHIP MIGHT MEAN MARRIAGE

O God,
you made me;
you redeemed me;
you called me to your service;
you gave me grace to begin to answer that call.

O God,
you made her;
you redeemed her;
you called her to your service;
you gave her grace to begin to answer that call.

You know that we are attracted to each other.
Help us to know whether your calling
in the case of each of us
specifically includes
a calling
to be united together
in your service.

WAR

I see the Beast of War
snarling in the television set.
Men crawling on their stomachs, like snakes in the grass, to shoot at other men.
Flame throwers, hand-grenades, tanks, bombers,
helicopters with machine-guns.
Anxious women running among the bullets
clutching strangely unperturbed children
and praying for safety.

And there are the corpses.
Bullet-smashed bundles of bone and bleeding flesh.
Men
who once were children at a mother's breast
on a day which to the mother was but yesterday.
Men killed by another mother's child.
The war has come into our living room today.
We have been to the war and we have seen it.
Lord, why do we have war?
Surely mankind is old enough and knows enough about history and diplomacy to be able to get along without it?
Where does war come from?
It comes from the clash of ideologies
between those, for example, who say that 'Capital must belong to the State', and those who say 'Every man has the right to own capital'.
And it comes too from the clash of cultures and races between people who have different coloured skins and racial origins. White fights black and blacks fight white.
Jew fights Arab, and Arab fights Jew.

A Hitler thinks his nation is the master-race to whom all should bow, and finds it the object of a world's revolt.
And war comes too from disputes over land,
about who owns what, and where.
For reasons like these
mankind puts up with War.
For a while it seemed that fear would bring reason.
If for no other reason than this
the atom-bomb seemed to be tolerable. But now it seems that men will fight whatever happens and we are faced with two dismal possibilities:
the extinction of all life in our own day and age;
or the continuation of non-nuclear wars like these,
ad infinitum,
unless
mankind can learn
a desire for peace strong enough to pay the price of peace.

A PRAYER ABOUT THE DEATH OF YOUNG PEOPLE

Lord
I am shocked
to see the reality of death.
To see it not as something comfortably remote,
taking place in the dim recesses of a great old age,
happening in the twilight of a nursing home
where it is expected and often desired.
I am shocked to see it as something which happens
on a day like today
to someone like me.
I haven't seen it in this light before —
as something happening to somebody intensely alive.
But somewhere, for someone just like me, death is always here and now.
And it bothers me that life should be unfulfilled,
and that you should permit it to be so.
How tragic that such a wonderful thing as life should be unfinished at its termination, incomplete when it is ended.
I have learned today
that terrible things happen — and that they happen all the time —
on a day like this, in a life like mine.
And I am saddened
and perplexed.
What does the Bible have to say to me about this problem?
The Bible is full of wars and fighting.
Its pages are strewn with the corpses of the young.
From Abel, to Jonathan, to Jesus
We see the young men slain.

Not only are children slaughtered, as they were by Herod around Bethlehem,
but in the Bible we read of them slaughtered before birth in the wombs of their mothers.
The Bible is not a pretty book.
That is why I turn to it now with hope. If it were a pretty book it would not have much to offer to this world.
It's good to see men like Abraham, Isaac, Jacob and David — men on whom the favour of the Lord rested — it's good to see them live to a ripe old age. It's good to see Job be faithful to God in his terrible trials
and reach great age with peace. It's good
to know of the great age of John, the beloved disciple. It's good to know that there is some connection between goodness and length of life. It's good, also, to know that the connection isn't a necessary one. For above all,
it's good to know that Jesus was able to accomplish His Father's will and cry 'It is finished' when He died. It's good to know that death for Him was an achievement. It's good to know that fulfilment can be achieved in the shortest of spans. It's good too to know of the Resurrection and of the power of God to do what ultimately and lastingly is right. In all these things
I begin to find my balance again.
Now I look death in the eyes once more
and measure myself against it.
And as I do so
there comes, reflected back to me, at once,
the challenge of
today.

THE LESSONS OF LEADERSHIP

One of the hardest lessons I've had to learn recently, Lord,
is that leadership doesn't bring appreciation:
not always, at any rate.

You know how it is that I have come to find this out for myself. I took on a job, that extra piece of
responsibility and leadership,
which I believe you required of me.
And
I really sweated over it. You know I did!
But when things didn't turn out too well
I was mercilessly criticized — flayed alive
by words, and looks . . .

Nobody mentioned my sacrifices of time and energy — or my work.
I was judged only on results. And the only
results people mentioned were
the bad ones. The good ones — and you know there were some — didn't even get a mention.

I have been thoroughly depressed about this.
I know, though, that it would be wrong and childish
for me to take the huff and pack everything in
just because of this.
For I am a Christian.
That means that I am one of those who have themselves persecuted Christ to the point where they have realized why
He did not strike back

but said
'Father forgive them . . .'
So now that I am, in this small way, misunderstood and unappreciated, help me to forgive.
And help me not to lose my nerve
but to become a more competent leader instead.
Help me to
see to it that more things go right
and fewer things go wrong.
And help me also to be more patient
with other leaders;
to be less critical, or when critical to be constructive;
certainly to be more helpful;
and to pray for them.
For now I know what it feels like.
It's a lonely, thankless business being a leader.
People can be jealous at your success, and nasty about your failure. Worst of all, some of them are only nice to you because of what they think they can get out of you.
I thank you Lord
that Jesus knew all about this problem, and that in all its aspects he mastered it.
And I thank you God, the leader of all true life, that leadership is your proper sphere, and that we can pray to you.
Help me to make you my model, and to receive your grace.
And so I pray for all the leaders of men and nations in their terrible responsibilities and opportunities. Help them, realistically — to make you their model, and to find in you their unfailing friend.
Bless them. Strengthen them. And give them friends on earth too.

Through Jesus Christ our Lord.

Amen.

A PRAYER FOR ALL LEADERS

O God
you are the Creator of all things.
Therefore
Whether the fact is acknowledged or not —
you are the rightful leader of those engaged in scientific research and scholarship.

Bless all those who explore creation —
those whose researches are into the physical universe;
those whose study is the mind of man;
those who seek to understand his history, societies and cultures.
Lead them all by their many paths towards the truth
and let there be light.

O God,
you are the King of Creation,
your will constitutes its laws.
You do not coerce. But neither may you be mocked.
And long before the last analysis we may know that
it is your law only which operates adequately
in the affairs of men.

You, therefore, alone are the true leader of governments —
only you are completely competent to guide the
politicians, economists and sociologists of the world.
Lead them, Lord, and make them willing to follow, so
that in your service
they may find freedom and peace for all men
including themselves.

O God,
you are Lord of the Church.
And, of all mankind, it alone claims
to be obedient to the God we see in Christ.
How badly it fails.
Help me to see that the failure of the Church is simply
my own personal failure writ large.
But although we fail we are staggered to see
how wonderfully
you continue to work your miracles through your
Church.
Guide church leaders, O God, and
lead your Church
into purity, unity, power and grace,
through Jesus Christ our Lord.

O God, you are the supreme visionary, judge, arbiter,
tactician, diplomat, politician, artist, craftsman, labour-
er.
You are the true leader of mankind.
Bless the leaders of the world, we pray.

MAKE ME A THINKER, GOD

Make me a thinker, God.
For it is the thinker who shapes the world.
Karl Marx, for example,
was a thinker . . .
His thought,
a mighty mixture of truth and error,
has changed the world — changed it both for good and ill.
But Jesus was a thinker too.
Help me to think His thoughts.
Help me to think them in the context of the mightiest ideas at work in the world today.
From ideas come ideologies,
and from the clash of ideologies comes (so often) war.
But in the last resort
ideas can only be overcome by better ideas,
ideas not worshipped as the truth, but made to serve love.
So make me a thinker, Lord. Make me your thinker.
And teach me to put my thoughts
clearly into the minds of men.

THE PUNY MIND

What a puny thing the mind is.
It attacks a problem
only to fall back exhausted every few minutes.
Its strength is measured by the number of times it can
pick itself up and try again,
in the number of times it can bring itself back
to the same hurdles.
As I pray to be made a thinker, Lord,
I pray for patience,
persistence,
strength.

A DOER OF THE WORD

A man of thought and speech and literacy —
no matter how deep his thought,
how clear his speech,
how clever his pen —
is not yet what man was designed by God to be.
Man was made for life. And life
involves action.
Therefore, God, please
make me more than a man of thought,
more than a man of talk:
make me also a doer of the word.

PART 3

UNDERSTANDING CHRISTMAS

I want to understand Christmas, Lord.
But it's hard to be dispassionate and objective in my approach to it.
It's hard to be 'scientific' about this time of year.
For so many of my thoughts about it
are touched and coloured by the huge delights of childhood and the glow which these have cast
like magic
about everything to do with it.
But Christmas
of course
is not a 'time of year'. Not really.
It is a corporate recollection
by believers
of the central fact of history:
that God became man.
And this is the heart-stopping, brain-numbing
fact
which is half illuminated
and half obscured
by our Christmas festivities.

BETHLEHEM

All day people had been arriving,
returning to their native town, the place from which
their fathers and their grandfathers had come,
going back to be taxed.
And so the town was crowded. And when night fell
it was crowded beyond its capacity.
Many homes were crammed with
holiday-minded relatives making the most of the required journey,
and talking about old times, old hopes.
The inns didn't have a spare bed, mattress, or sleeping
space.
Even the stables behind the inns
were occupied by more than animals.

Night thickened
and the lines of tethered asses and hobbled camels
settled slowly into stillness. Even the dogs,
scavenging among the plentiful rubbish of the day,
gradually disappeared, replete, and ready for a
sheltered spot.

And
all was still.
But in one stable, among the animals, there was
a small bustle of urgent, anxious, controlled activity,
until to one young mother
a son was born.
And this was good news of a new kind
to all sorts of people.
It was good news for the restless minds

of wise men from the thoughtful East
who knelt before this answer to their questionings, and rejoiced
that reason and much learning
now united them with shepherds of the field,
for whom the heavens were brighter and the path more straight.
There was great gladness there as Christmas gifts were offered —
the precious, simple gifts of peasant folk
and the treasures of the wise.

Now,
in imagination and devotion,
all God's children gather here to see.
And this day I am with them.

Thank you Lord
for loving us so much
as to be practical, definite, specific in the way in which you come to us.
Thank you for finding the language which all men can understand
and thank you
for the heart-breaking humility
at the centre of your Majesty.
That is why
at the Name of Jesus, every knee shall bow.

CHRISTMAS CARDS AND PRESENTS

It's great fun, of course, God,
or at least it used to be
when it wasn't so much work!
But I must admit that it's reaching such proportions now that the work outweighs the fun.
If I'm to be completely honest I shall have to admit that I'm more than a little fed up with it.
It's so hard to remember everybody. It all costs so much money. It all takes so much time and energy.
What is the meaning of it?
You were born at Christmas!
At least we have chosen to remember your birth at a time we have *called* 'Christmas'.
It's the best we can do. It's a good idea.
And you came to live, and to give . . .
and to make man at one with God, and all men at one with each other in God.
But the people I love are scattered all over the place.
There are so many, and we never seem to get together in one place at one time.
But just the same we can be united in spirit. And we can send a gift or card, so that each house can be like a heart sending out and taking in the life blood of the company to which we belong.

A PRAYER BEFORE GOING CAROL SINGING

O God, the sky is dark, and the streets are empty and cold.
But there are lights in the windows, and there is a light in our hearts.
Accept the gladness of our songs in these dark and chilly streets, and may the people who hear us rejoice with us.
May we provide a happy memory for small children going to bed; may we give a moment's rest to overworked parents; may we be a joy and comfort to those who feel that the Christmas spirit is passing them by; and for those who scorn the Christmas spirit, may we be messengers of Him whose Spirit it truly is. Grant O Lord that tonight many may know the presence of Christ because they hear us sing.

A PRAYER AFTER CAROL SINGING

Thank you, Lord, for these warm hearts on this cold night.
Thank you for all who have sung, all who have listened, all who have thought of you, all who have given to you, and all who have been drawn more closely together.
Thank you for these carols, old and new.
Thank you above all for the one about whom they were written, the One about whom we have been singing, the One, whom with you, Father, and the Holy Spirit, we adore, now and forever.
Amen.

LENT

As the days lengthen
and the earth spends longer in the light of day
grant that I may spend longer in the light of your presence,
O Lord.
And may those seeds of your Word,
which have been long buried within me,
grow,
like everything around us,
into
love for you,
and love for people;
to become
a visible declaration of
your Lordship in my life.
Grant, Father, that this Lent there may be a springtime
for my life in Christ.

GOOD FRIDAY

There's something about this day,
something that no other day has got.
It stands alone.
It has stood alone for nearly two thousand years.
It will stand alone for all time.
Wherever I go today,
whatever I do
there is the thought of Golgotha —
the place of a skull —
and the ceremonial murder of the Son of God,
man's worst against God's best,
man's sin upon God's love,
the greatest evil against the greatest good,
Christ impaled.
And the curious, malicious, muddled,
triumphant, sorrowful
mixture of men
looking on.
The long fierce hours dragged darkly on
their shadows lengthening into this very day until
they touch my heart.
Some people wash their cars this morning
but at nine they had nailed Him to the tree.
Some people lie till noon,
but it had been thirty hours since He slept.
The crowds prepare for the holiday football match,
giving their rattles a preliminary shake
and stopping at the local near the gates.
By then had come a darkness on the earth.
Now as then most people do not know what really holds
the stage of human history.

So Jesus died for men:
for the car-washers, and the lie-abeds,
the lusty lads in football boots, the cheerful crowds,
and even for the ref.
Forgetfully, the world goes on its way.
Jesus with determination dies.
'The just for the unjust
that He might bring us to God.'
And I will watch with Him
naming the sins of mine which put Him there,
and seeing a portrait of myself
in the pain God bears
in bringing me
to Himself.

THE DAY AFTER GOOD FRIDAY

This is the one day in the whole year when we remember a dead Christ.
That is a contradiction in terms, it's true: for
Christ is life; how then can He be dead?
But yet the hard fact remains that one dark day He died.
And His disciples fled, and hid themselves for fear of the Jews.
And on the day after His murder
the corpse of Jesus lay
wrapped in its shroud, solitary and chill,
in the dark
behind the cold and massive stone, where
no light, no sound, no air, no warmth, no sign or hint of life could find its way.
There were just a few cubic yards of
silence
surrounding the 'nothingness' of the corpse.
Jesus emptied Himself. He was one with God but emptied Himself of all the rights and privileges of Deity and became a man. And as a man He emptied Himself again
and died.
He being rich became poor. He being poor became nothing.
And on this day we remember the nothingness of Christ,
and the reason for it.
Ourselves.
There would have been little peace in the stillness of Jerusalem on the day which we remember today.

Certainly
the murderers of Christ would have had no peace, while they laid the mantle of 'political necessity' like a shroud upon their conscience. The wife of Pilate perhaps would dream again her dream and cry 'have thou nothing to do with that just man!' And Pilate would pace the judgment hall, harrassed and alone. The disciples would have no peace, for they had deserted their Lord in His hour of need, and even now were still afraid that the cross might be their destiny as well. Mary would have no peace for she had seen on the cross the baby she had borne and reared and loved.
But there were two men, perhaps, who knew
something approaching peace — the only kind of peace possible on that day. For when Jesus died two secret disciples came forward and let it be known that they were His.
Joseph of Arimathaea, and Nicodemus.
For them
the torture of a secret allegiance was over.
The cross had claimed its victory. They were His.
Jesus died for us. Because of us, and on our behalf.
On this day there can be no peace for us but this:
the peace of being seen by all men
to be His.

EASTER MORNING

As morning comes
something is different.
The women hurry to their leader's grave
anxious
to care for the body placed out of bounds till now
by Sabbath law. But
as they approach
something there is different, and
at the grave
there is shock:
unimagineable, unguessable, physical, convulsive.
The grave is empty.
Empty of all but light.
And that light
as complete
as the darkness which had reigned
till now.
Yesterday's insane contradiction
was the dead body of the Lord of Life.
Today's miraculous sanity
rises
in their mind at the summons of
the risen body of
the risen Lord.

COULD IT BE TRUE?

The tomb was empty!
That was the point. It was *empty!*
And all the people who desperately needed to prove
that Jesus was dead,
and scotch the rumour of His resurrection,
could not produce the body.
The tomb was empty. And those
who wished it otherwise,
could not make it so.
It therefore follows
that one of two things must be true.
Either
the body of Jesus had been stolen,
or
Jesus was risen from the dead.
But who could have stolen it?
The disciples?
Had they stolen it in order to propagate a
fiction,
and to found a
false faith?
That theory comes within the bounds of possibility.
But it is a possibility almost impossible to
believe.
For one day earlier the disciples had been terrified and
in hiding.
Could they then have rallied themselves from
such a demoralized state and
organized
a raid of such daring?
For the theft of such a body,

when the interest of a whole nation was centred upon it,
and a heavily armed guard was set around it,
would require qualities of spirit, mind and nerve
which they could not be expected to
muster at such a time. Besides,
after this day the disciples became changed men —
triumphant, victorious, self-assured.
From this day they went on to risk their lives
in the service of this Christ.
Would they have done so as a consequence of
a lie
which they had themselves
manufactured?
The whole proposition seems to be a
psychological impossibility.
If the disciples had stolen the body they were the
greatest actors, and the most callous confidence
tricksters
of all time,
and they did not act or speak or live like that.
Could the body then have been stolen by
professional grave-robbers?
Again that's possible. But what an odd robber it would
be to make an attempt upon a guarded grave
containing the body of someone executed as a felon,
and
therefore
without the treasures
which robbers seek to get.
Above all, how odd to steal the body, instead of the
clothes —
for they alone could be of any value to them.
In this case it was the body which was gone and the

clothes which remained.
It could not have been grave-robbers.
Certainly it would not have been stolen by the Romans!
All they wanted was civil order and peace.
This, they thought, they had secured.
That leaves the Jews. Could they have done it?
If they had it raises the question why?
Why should they do so, when it was they who had asked that a guard be set upon the grave?
And why, if it had been them, did they not then
scotch the rumour
by producing the body and saying:
'He is not risen — look we have his body here'?

The tomb was empty. Empty. And it cannot fairly be thought that
the body was stolen.
And that means that we must conclude that
He was
raised from the dead.

Is it possible?

Why should it not be? It cannot in any way
be said to be
contrary to reason.
Reason *cannot* say that the Resurrection is *impossible!*
All reason can do is to note that, so far as we know,
the event is unique.
But for a thing to be unique does not make that thing contrary to reason.
The Resurrection is not an event subject to the judgment of reason as such.

It is quite simply a matter of
observation:
observation by eye-witnesses whom
we either believe or disbelieve.
Belief in the Resurrection then is not belief in a
proposition.
It is acceptance of observed fact.
And for me the disciples are believable. They are
credible witnesses.
And since I accept them as such I also accept their
statement.
I accept the fact to which they bear witness.
I believe that Jesus Christ rose from the dead.

THE ASCENSION

He had been appearing to them,
off and on,
for nearly six weeks now.
They had got used to living with the knowledge
that He was risen,
and that at any moment He might
materialize at their side.
They grew to know that —
whether seen or unseen —
the Lord was at hand — as near to them, indeed, as
their own hands.
Now He led them off,
as He done so often before,
for a long walk into the country — 'far from the madd-
ing crowd' — away up a mountain side, to its very top.
And there
with great energy, and great authority,
He spoke to them.
'All the power in and behind creation has been made
part of me,' He said. 'Now, you are to go
into all places,
and preach the gospel to everybody.
Baptize them.
Everything that I have taught you, you are to teach
them.
And be sure of this:
I am with you always.'
A great sun-filled cloud covered the mountain-top with
its golden mist. And when it dispersed
the Lord was gone.
He was nowhere to be found on earth;

it was clear to the disciples that He was being parted from them. So they concluded that now the Lord had been received into heaven.

And so they returned to Jerusalem
to wait, with great expectancy, and desire —
for God's next move.

HE ASCENDED INTO HEAVEN

Heaven is the starting place of all creation, and
the destination of all that is redeemed by God.
It is also, the eternal and contemporary dwelling place
of the Almighty.
And since
God existed
in the fullness of His Being
before Creation
Heaven itself also existed *before* Creation. Therefore Heaven cannot be a *part of* the physical universe, and cannot be a specific location somewhere in space.
Our thoughts, and therefore our words, are limited in their scope, and so we *call* Heaven a 'place'. It's a real help to do so. But Heaven is the reality from which life and all creation springs. And Jesus 'ascended into Heaven'. He returned to the starting place, and destination, of God's purposes, which is the sphere of absolute reality.
How wonderful, Lord,
that you should leave the disciples to stand on their own feet.
How wonderful,
that you should trust them to set off on their own.
How wonderful,
that you should not want to keep them
(so to speak)
tied to your apron strings,
but were ready to allow them, in all their imperfection,
to stand for and represent
you
in the world.

This was their graduation day.
Now they were as ready for their job as you could make them —
save for one thing only:
the gift of the Spirit
which would give
power to their knowledge, and life to their words.

PENTECOST

Every day they had been in the Temple
worshipping and praising God.
Jesus had left them, it was true.
But He had left them with a promise.
And this, they knew, would be fulfilled, and its fulfilment
would make Him real as never before,
would make life real, as never before;
would widen and develop their powers to the fullest extent, and would give them powers they had not previously possessed.
They would receive the Promise, which would integrate their personalities,
bringing into mighty harmony
their will, their desires, their emotions, their thoughts,
making them whole, and
making them more completely human
through making them more like Jesus.
And so they waited.
And when they were
'All
with one consent
in one place'
there came the sound as of rushing mighty wind
and the fire fell.
It came to each one individually.
It came to all of them corporately.
Their individual fulfilment
meant their complete fellowship and interdependence.
And as they became open to God —
to each other —

to all mankind —
they understood, as never before,
the thoughts of men,
entered into
the speech of all nations and
spoke the universal language of God.
The streets became their pulpit,
everybody became their audience,
and in that day alone
three thousand men changed their minds
about Jesus
and became followers of Him.

A PRAYER FOR THE HOLY SPIRIT

Show us Jesus as He is, O Lord.
May we see Him as the first disciples saw Him.
May He be as real to us as He was on earth to them.
Bring us to the Cross;
may we see what it meant for Him
and what it means for us.
Show to us the empty tomb and
may the Resurrection be as much a matter of observation as of faith.
May we see Christ to be Lord and God,
and know that all the power in the universe
is in Him.
Do these things for us Lord
for when they are done we shall be ready
for the gift of the Holy Spirit.
We shall be open to you,
to each other,
to the world.
We shall be ready for there to be in our lives
a process of unlimited change.
So may all the secret and devious paths of our minds
become straight.
And may we live in the light as members one of
another,
our lives fulfilled individually
and fused together within
the marvellous fellowship of your Son.
And so may we hear what others say when they speak.
And may we speak what all the world shall understand.
And grant Lord that the world may listen, believe and
be changed.

'HE SHALL COME AGAIN WITH GLORY'

Considering that I have said these words so often
in church
it's amazing
that I've never taken them very seriously.
How seriously are we meant to take them?
It's certainly the case that the first disciples took them very seriously indeed.
According to the Book of Acts
the first thing that the disciples heard after the ascension of Christ was the promise of His return.
And in His own teaching it seems quite clear
that Jesus frequently spoke about His second coming.
I see that this event is referred to over two hundred times in the New Testament.
The book is full of it.
So far as the Bible, is concerned then —
so far as the Creeds are concerned then —
so far as the Church is concerned then
the whole idea of Christ's second coming is not an optional extra to which, out of courtesy, we do no more than tip our hats in the creed . . .
It is something of
paramount importance. And amongst other things it must be something in which my own ordinary life must one day be involved.
And yet it is has been so foreign to my way of thinking.
It makes me think of cranks and queer religious sects.
And indeed it's just the sort of idea which can be so easily distorted
by cranks within the Church
and by critics outside it.

What does the Bible tell us about it?
That it will be sudden, universal, irreversible.
Something beyond our powers either to forecast or to stop.
It will be something absolutely just, right, fair and good.
It will be a thing of great gladness for those who love God.
It will be a day of terror and destruction for those who worship themselves.
In every respect.
It will be a day of complete reality
when the fictions with which we surround ourselves and cloud our minds are dispersed
and we see God and ourselves as we truly are
and at last understand everything.